KU-525-653

What Do
LEVERS Do?

David Glover

www.heinemann.co.uk/library
Visit our website to find out more information about Heinemann Library books.

To order:
 Phone 44 (0) 1865 888066
Send a fax to 44 (0) 1865 314091
 Visit the Heinemann Bookshop at www.heinemann.co.uk/library to browse our
catalogue and order online.

First published in Great Britain by Heinemann Library,
Halley Court, Jordan Hill, Oxford OX2 8EJ, part
of Harcourt Education. Heinemann is a registered
trademark of Harcourt Education Ltd.

© Harcourt Education Ltd 1996, 2006
The moral right of the proprietor has been asserted.

Editorial: Clare Lewis and Katie Shepherd
Design: Victoria Bevan and Q2A Creative
Illustrations: Barry Atkinson (p15), Douglas Hall (pp18,
19), Tony Kenyon (pp5, 9), and Ray Straw (p12)
Picture Research: Mica Brancic
Production: Helen McCreath
Printed and bound in China by WKT Company
Limited

10 digit ISBN 0 431 06406 7
13 digit ISBN 978 0 431 06406 2
10 09 08 07 06
10 9 8 7 6 5 4 3 2 1

British Library Cataloguing in Publication Data
Glover, David
What do levers do? - 2nd Edition
621.8'2
A full catalogue record for this book is available from
the British Library.

Acknowledgements
The publishers would like to thank the following for
permission to reproduce photographs: Trevor Clifford
pp1, 4, 6, 7, 8, 9, 10, 11, 12, 14, 15, 21; Collections/
Keith Pritchard p16; Spectrum Colour Library p18;
Tony Stone Images p17; Zefa p13.

Cover photograph reproduced with permission of
Alamy.

The publishers would like to thank Angela Royston for
her assistance in the preparation of this book.

Every effort has been made to contact copyright
holders of any material reproduced in this book. Any
omissions will be rectified in subsequent printings if
notice is given to the publishers.

The paper used to print this book comes from
sustainable resources.

Any words appearing in the text in bold, **like this**, are
explained in the Glossary

Contents

What are levers?

A lever is a rod or bar that makes things move. A see-saw is a lever. It has a **pivot** in the middle where it turns. If you push down on one end of a see-saw, the other end goes up.

A light person can balance a heavy person on a see-saw. The heavier person must sit nearer to the pivot.

pivot

This plank is a lever. It pivots at one end. You can use a lever to lift a heavy **load** with a small **effort**, if the load is near the pivot.

Levers do many different jobs inside machines. They change pushes into pulls and they balance weights. Levers also move big loads with little effort.

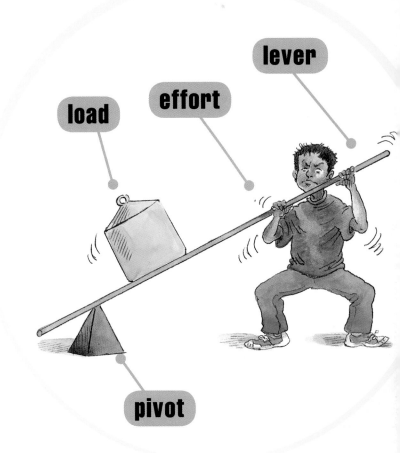

load

effort

lever

pivot

FACT FILE Lever words

Pivot: the place where the lever turns.
Effort: the push or pull that makes a lever work.
Load: the weight that the lever lifts.

Openers

Have you ever opened a tin with the handle of a spoon? The lid fits too tightly to open with your fingers. But when you use the spoon to open the tin, the lid comes off easily.

The spoon handle is the lever. Your hand makes the **effort**. The stiff lid is the **load**. The place where the handle rests on the edge of the tin is the **pivot**.

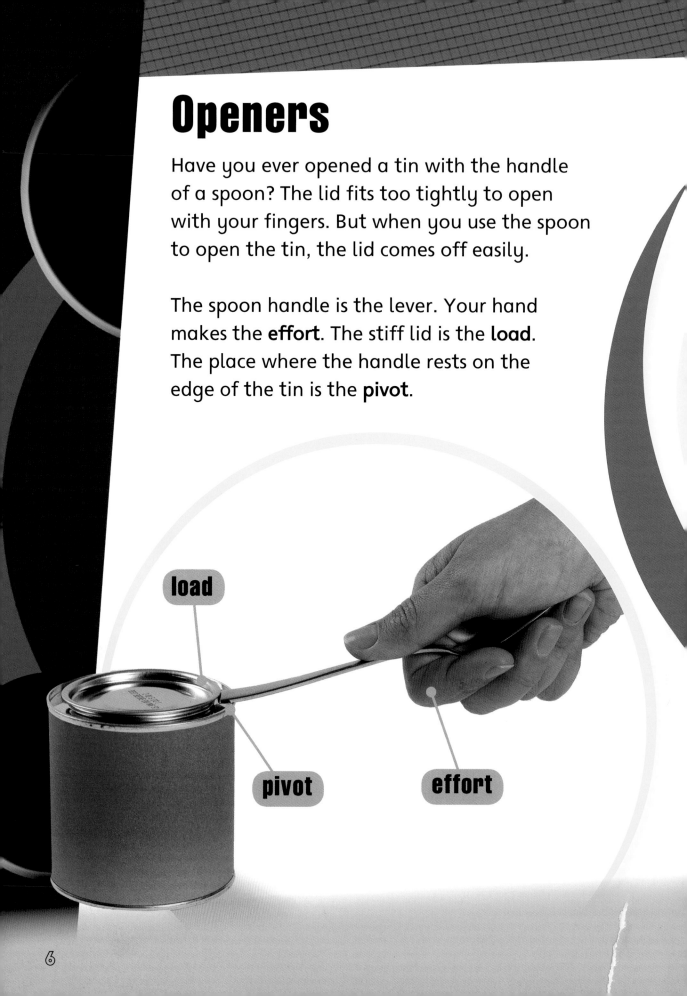

load

pivot

effort

Magnify your strength!

Levers can magnify your strength. They increase the effect of your strength. With a lever you can push or pull much harder than you can with your bare hands. This is why levers are so useful.

A bottle opener is also a lever. It pivots on the bottle top. Your effort as you lift the end of the opener levers the bottle top off.

Barrows

A barrow works as a lever to lift heavy **loads**. A gardener's wheelbarrow **pivots** around the wheel. The gardener's **effort** on the handles is farther away from the pivot than the load. The gardener can lift more in a barrow than in her bare arms.

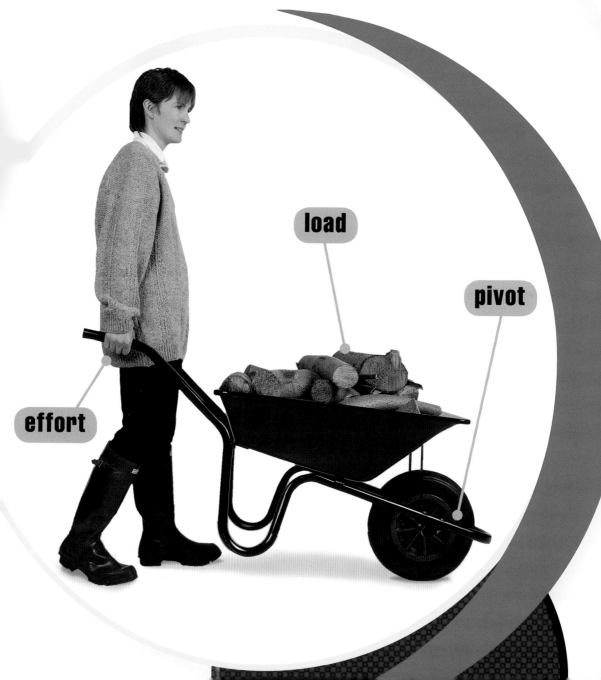

load

pivot

effort

This porter's barrow has long handles. It levers heavy cases off the ground. When the cases rest over the wheels, the porter can balance them with little effort.

Moving the world!

In ancient Greece, the scientist Archimedes knew that levers could magnify strength. He said, "Give me a long enough lever and I will move the world!"

Tools

You are not strong enough to pull out a nail with your fingers. But you can lever it out with a **claw hammer**. When you pull on the handle the hammer **pivots** on its head. The claws grip the nail and drag it out of the wood.

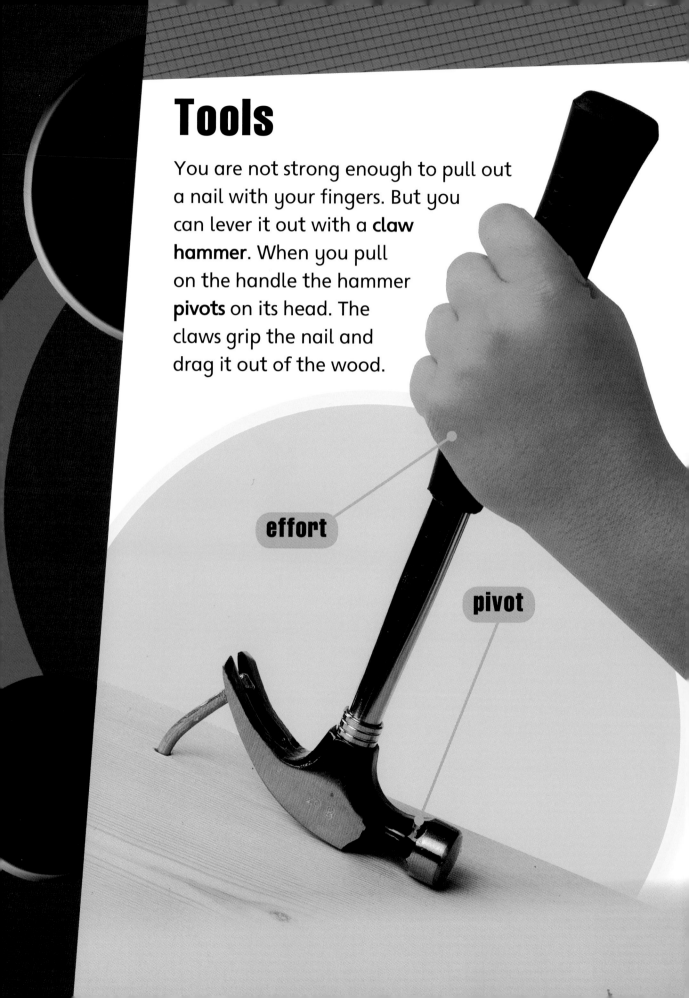

effort

pivot

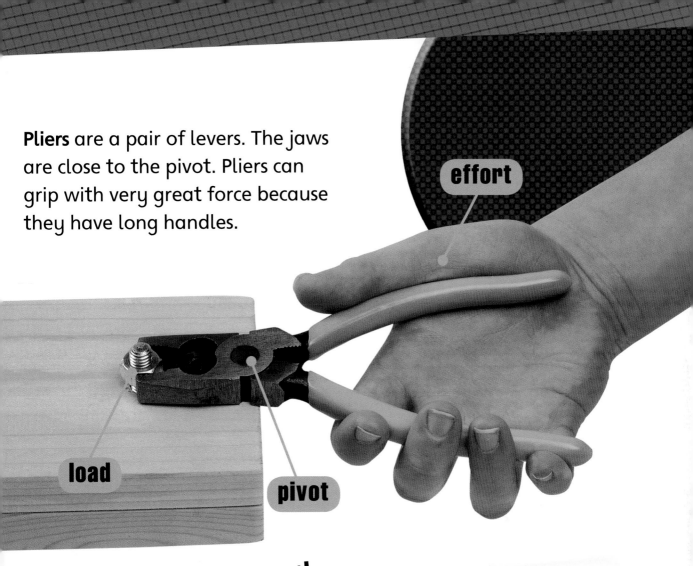

Pliers are a pair of levers. The jaws are close to the pivot. Pliers can grip with very great force because they have long handles.

effort

load

pivot

Jaw power!

Your jaws are a pair of levers. They work like pliers. Your back teeth are closer to the hinge of your jaws than your front teeth, so they can bite harder. That is why it is easier to crunch a carrot with your back teeth.

Crackers and cutters

Nutcrackers are a pair of levers with a **pivot** at one end. You can prove that they **magnify** your strength. First, try cracking a hard nut between your fingers. Unless you are superman you will not be able to. Now use the nutcrackers – it will make a big difference!

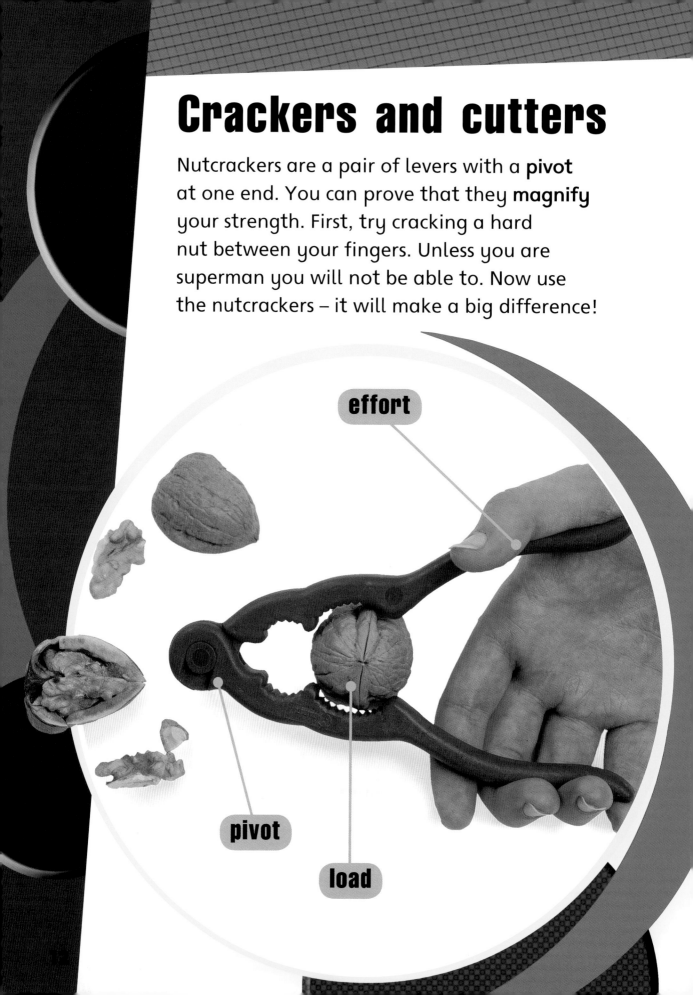

effort

pivot

load

The long handles on these cutters magnify the **effort** from your arms. They can snip through thick branches. With cutters like this you can even cut through metal bars.

Cracking chimps!

Chimpanzees can crack nuts with stones. But the human being is the only animal to use levers.

Balances

This toy balance is a lever, just like a see-saw. You can experiment to see how far from the **pivot** you have to put different weights in order to make them balance.

Can you balance two weights on one side with one weight on the other side? The weight on its own must be twice as far from the pivot to make it work.

These kitchen scales use a lever to find when the weights are balanced. If you want to weigh some apples you put the apples in one pan. Next you add the weights to the other pan. If the apples weigh more than the weights, their pan stays down. If the weights weigh more, the apples go up. If the weights are equal, the pans are exactly balanced.

FACT FILE "Feather weight"

A good balance is very accurate. The weight of one feather is enough to "tip the balance" one way or the other.

feather

Bridges

This bridge has to be lifted out of the way to let a boat pass by. It is fixed to a lever. When one end of the lever arm is pulled down, the other end pulls the bridge up into the air.

There is a heavy weight on one end of the lever arm. This weight balances most of the weight of the bridge. A person can lift the bridge with just a little extra **effort**.

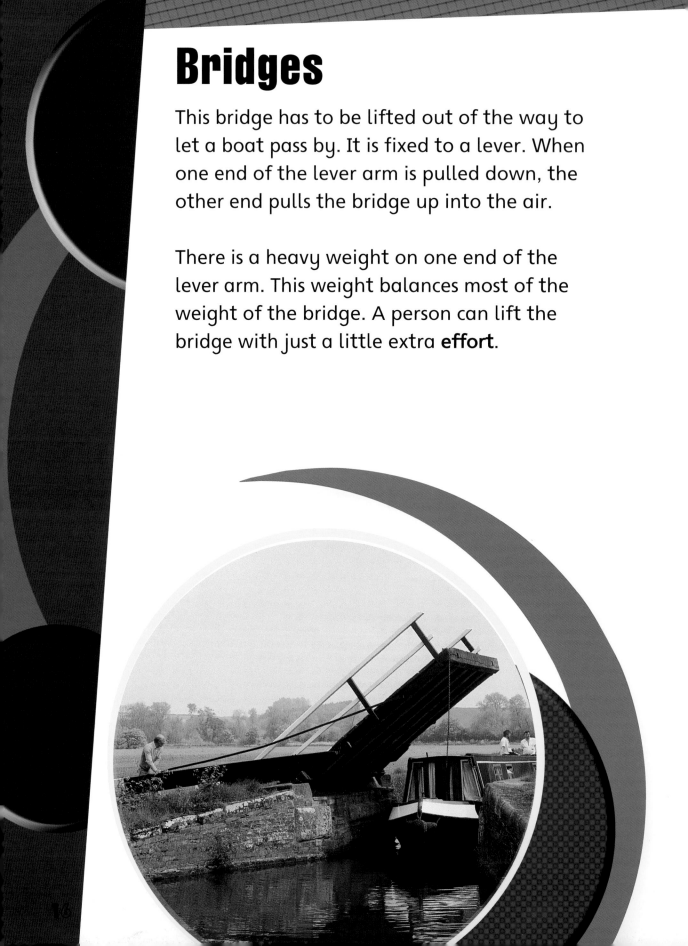

Tower Bridge in London is a lever bridge. Its decks weigh about 1,000 tonnes. They are balanced by huge weights. When a ship needs to pass under the bridge, electric **motors** lift up the decks.

FACT FILE **Lifting the bridge**

The levers of Tower Bridge are so carefully balanced that they can be lifted by a small motor. The motor is the same size as the motor inside a lawn mower.

Rods and oars

An **angler** uses levers, because a fishing rod is a lever. He uses one hand as **pivot** and the other one for the **effort**. Small movements of his hands are **magnified** by the long rod. When the angler gets a bite he can move his rod very quickly.

load

effort

pivot

The oars on a rowing boat are levers too. You pull on the oars to lever the boat through the water. The oars pivot in the **rowlocks**.

Oar power!

Some ancient warships called galleys had more than 100 oars. Each oar was pulled by one man.

effort

load

rowlock (pivot)

Brakes

Could you stop a heavy cart like this with one hand? The answer is yes, if you use a brake lever. The lever pushes a wooden block on to the wheel. **Friction** slows the wheel down. Friction is the force that stops things from sliding easily.

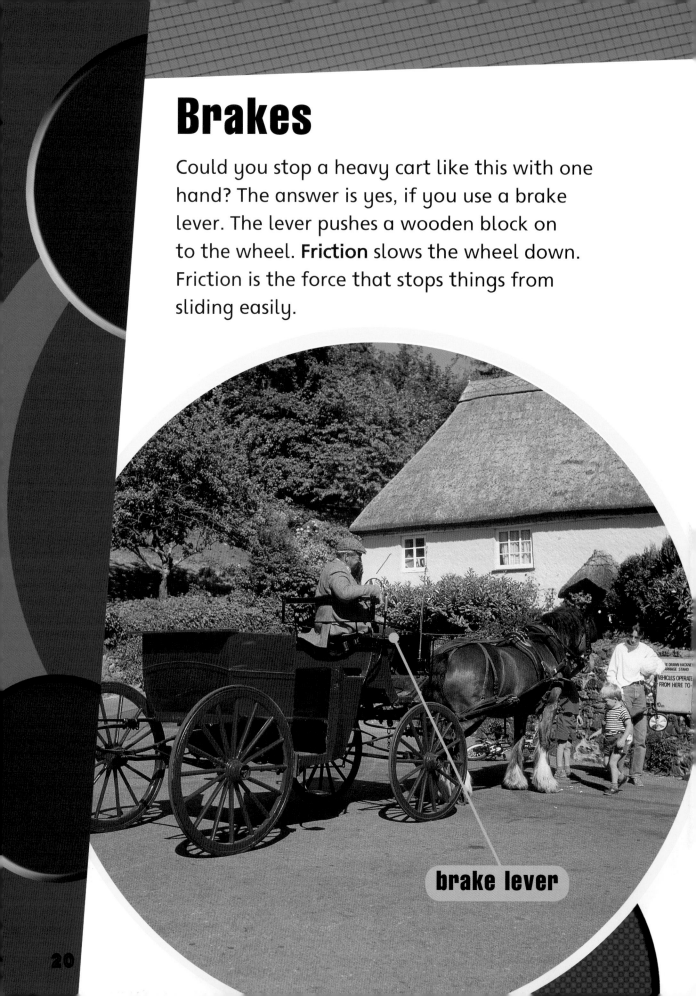

brake lever

Smoking brakes

Friction can make brakes so hot that they smoke or even catch fire!

The brake levers on a bicycle pull on wires. The wires pull on levers that are fixed to the frame near the wheels. These levers push rubber brake blocks onto the wheel to slow down the bicycle.

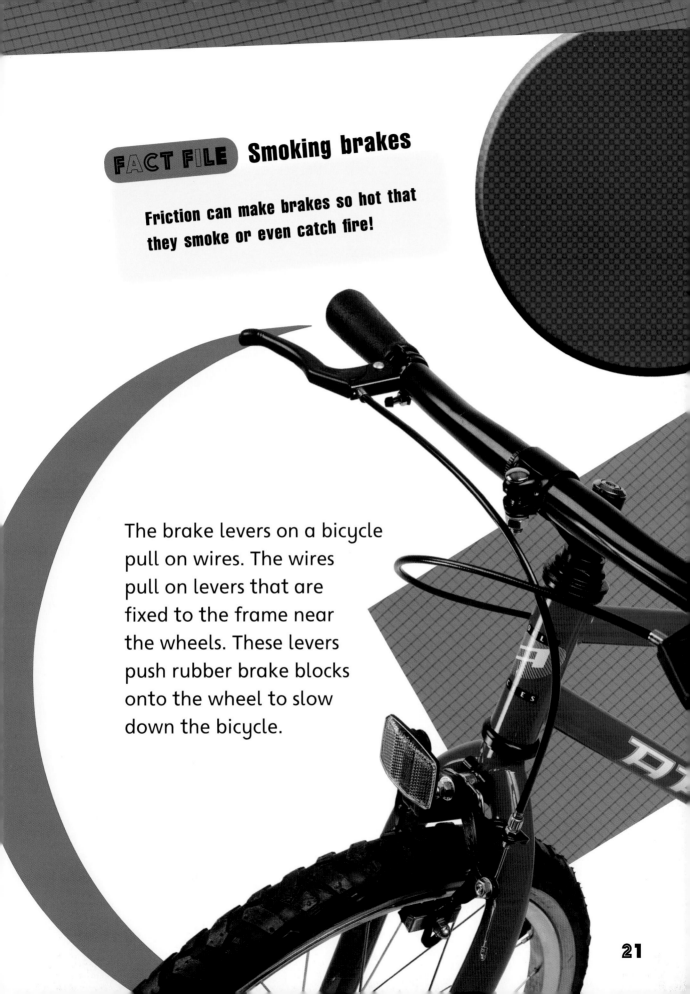

Activities

Which is the best lever?

1. Balance a long ruler over a pivot, such as a block of wood.
2. Rest another piece of wood on one end.
3. Push down on the other end of the ruler to lever up the wood.
4. Repeat this, using a standard (30cm) ruler. Then use a short (15cm) ruler.

Which ruler makes the best lever?

Make it balance

1. Make a balanced seesaw using a ruler and a pivot.
2. Put a weight on one end and two weights on the other end. What happens?
3. Move the heavy weights towards the pivot until the see-saw balances again.
4. Repeat this using different numbers of weights on the heavier end.

This is explained on pages 4 and 14.

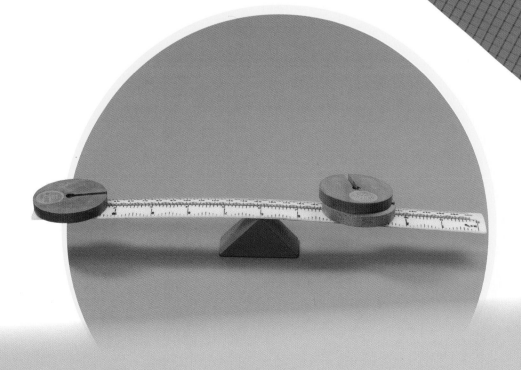

Glossary

angler Someone who uses a rod and line to catch fish.

claw hammer A hammer with two claws on the back of the head.

effort The push or pull you use to move something.

friction The drag or force that stops one thing sliding over another smoothly.

load Something, usually heavy, that you are trying to move.

magnified Made bigger.

motor A machine that uses electricity or fuels such as petrol or coal to make things move.

pivot The place around which a lever turns.

pliers Gripping tools with jaws which you can close by squeezing a pair of handles.

rowlocks The grips on the sides of a boat which hold the oars in place as you row.

Index